From Idea to Success

Kevin Myers

Kevin Myers

Legal and legal data
Copyright holder: © Sebastian Mendoza Gomez

Author: © Sebastian Mendoza Gomez
Category: Business

First edition

INDEX

Kevin Myers

Introduction to the Project Development Process

Developing a successful project can be exciting and challenging at the same time. Imagine having a great idea in mind and turning it into something tangible and successful in the real world. This is precisely what the project development process entails: taking an initial idea and bringing it to reality effectively and efficiently.

At its core, a project is a planned and coordinated effort to achieve a specific objective within certain parameters, such as time, resources, and scope. It can range from creating a new product to organizing a major event or implementing a significant change in an organization.

Project development typically begins with the identification of a need or opportunity. This first stage is crucial, as it establishes the foundation on which the entire project will be built. This is where the initial idea is generated, its feasibility is evaluated and it is decided if it is viable to turn it into a complete project.

Once the idea is clear and it has been decided to move forward, the planning phase begins. This is where specific project objectives are defined, a detailed plan is created, and roles and responsibilities are assigned to team members. Planning not only involves setting clear goals, but also estimating the resources needed, possible risks and how they will be managed, as well as establishing a realistic schedule.

With the plan in place, the execution phase follows. This involves carrying out activities as planned, coordinating team work, managing resources, and making adjustments as necessary. Execution is an active and dynamic stage, where ideas become reality and day-to-day challenges are faced.

Throughout the project development process, communication plays a fundamental role. It is crucial to keep all stakeholders informed and aligned, from the internal team to customers or end users. Effective communication helps avoid misunderstandings, resolve problems quickly, and maintain team motivation and commitment.

In addition to execution, it is vital to monitor and control the progress of the project. This involves regularly tracking milestones achieved, comparing progress with the initial plan, and taking corrective action if necessary. Risk management is also an integral part of the process, as it allows you to anticipate potential problems and be prepared to handle them without compromising the ultimate goal of the project.

Finally, each project concludes with a closure and evaluation phase. This is where the results obtained are reviewed, what went well is analyzed and what could be improved for future projects. It is a time to celebrate team achievements, learn from experiences and prepare for new challenges.

In short, the project development process is an exciting journey that involves transforming ideas into reality through meticulous planning, efficient execution, and continuous evaluation. It is a combination of creativity, organization and teamwork that allows us to achieve objectives and make business dreams come true.

Definition and Selection of the Initial Idea

When it comes to starting a project, it all starts with an idea. This initial idea is like the seed from which the entire project will grow. It can arise from different places: an identified need in the market, a sudden inspiration or even a solution to an existing problem. The important thing is that the idea has the potential to become something meaningful and viable.

The first task is to clearly define the idea. This involves describing what exactly you want to achieve with the project. What is the main purpose? What problem will it solve or what need will it satisfy? The more specific and clear the initial definition, the easier it will be to communicate and develop later.

Once the idea is defined, it is time to evaluate its viability. This means considering several aspects: Is there a market for this idea? Is there demand or interest for the product or service you plan to offer? Is it feasible from a technical and economic point of view? Conducting an initial analysis can help determine if the idea has the potential to become a successful project.

The selection of the idea also involves evaluating its alignment with the strategic objectives and values of the organization or the team that will carry out the project. Does the idea contribute to the growth or long-term goals of the company? Does it align with the team's mission and vision? These aspects are crucial to ensure that the selected idea is not only viable, but also consistent with the overall direction of the business.

It is important to keep in mind that not all initial ideas will be viable or suitable to become full-fledged projects. Some ideas may need to be adjusted, combined with others, or even discarded entirely. The ability to objectively evaluate and make informed decisions is essential in this selection process.

Finally, creativity and innovation play a key role in generating initial ideas. Often the best ideas come when you foster a creative environment and allow for outside-the-box thinking. Don't be afraid to explore different approaches or consider ideas that may seem risky at first.

Sometimes, those innovative ideas are what lead to the most successful projects.

In short, defining and selecting the initial idea is the first exciting and crucial step on the path to a successful project. It requires clarity, feasibility assessment, strategic alignment, and a healthy dose of creativity. It is the starting point where a simple idea can be transformed into a real opportunity to make a difference in the business world.

Market Analysis and Viability

When you have a great idea for a project, the next important step is to understand the market where you are going to launch it. Market analysis is like researching the land before building a house: it gives you a clear idea of who your potential customers are, what they are looking for, and how you can position yourself effectively.

The first step in market analysis is to identify your target audience. Who are the people or companies that could be interested in your product or service? This involves understanding their demographic characteristics (such as age, gender, location), purchasing behaviors, and specific needs that your idea could satisfy.

Once you know your target audience, it is crucial to research your competitors. Who else is offering something similar on the market? What are they doing right and what could they be leaving out? Analyzing the competition helps you identify opportunities and areas where you can differentiate yourself to stand out from the crowd.

In addition to studying the competition, it is important to analyze market trends. This involves understanding how the market is evolving in terms of demand for products or services similar to yours, changes in consumer preferences, technological advances or other factors that may influence your project.

Another key aspect of market analysis is evaluating the economic viability of your idea. This includes estimating the costs involved in producing, distributing and marketing your product or service, as well as determining the price at which you could sell it and how much you could earn. It is essential to ensure that there is a balance between costs and potential revenues for the project to be profitable.

In addition to economic aspects, it is also essential to consider legal and regulatory aspects. Depending on your industry and location, there may be specific regulations you must comply with, such as licenses, permits, or quality standards. Ignoring these aspects could lead to legal complications that could seriously affect the viability of your project.

In summary, market and feasibility analysis is a crucial phase in the development of any project. It provides a solid foundation for making informed and strategic decisions that maximize opportunities for success. By understanding your audience, studying the competition, staying aware of market trends, and evaluating economic and legal feasibility, you will be better prepared to successfully take your idea from paper to market.

Planning Strategy and Objectives

When it comes to carrying out a project, planning is key. It's like drawing a detailed map that will guide you from point A (your initial idea) to point B (the success of the project). The planning strategy involves establishing a series of steps and clear goals that will help you stay on track and achieve your goals efficiently.

The first step in the planning strategy is to define the project objectives clearly and specifically. What exactly do you want to achieve at the end of the project? Setting specific goals helps you maintain focus and measure progress along the way.

Once you have clear objectives, it's time to create a detailed plan. This involves breaking the project down into smaller tasks and assigning specific resources and time to each one. A good plan not only includes what to do, but also who will be responsible for each task and how the team's efforts will be coordinated.

During planning, it is also important to consider any potential obstacles or risks that could arise along the way. This allows you to anticipate potential problems and develop mitigation or contingency strategies to handle them if they occur. Preparation for the unexpected is key to keeping the project on track without major setbacks.

Another crucial aspect of the planning strategy is establishing a realistic calendar or schedule. This helps you manage time effectively and ensure that all tasks are completed at the right time. It is important to be realistic with deadlines and consider any external factors that may affect the progress of the project.

In addition to short-term planning, it is beneficial to take a long-term view. This involves not only meeting the immediate objectives of the project, but also considering how it might evolve in the future and how it might integrate with other larger projects or initiatives within the organization.

Finally, the planning strategy must be flexible. As you progress through the project, necessary changes or adjustments may arise. Being able to adapt to new circumstances and make informed decisions on the fly is critical to maintaining success over time.

In short, an effective planning strategy is essential to the success of any project. From setting clear objectives and developing a detailed plan to anticipating risks and maintaining flexibility, each step helps ensure the project moves efficiently toward completion. With a good planning strategy, you are better prepared to face the challenges and take advantage of the opportunities that arise on the path to success.

Building an Effective Team

When it comes to carrying out a project, the team you build is critical to success. Imagine you're building a sports team: you need the right players in the right positions to maximize your chances of winning. Similarly, building an effective team involves bringing together people with complementary skills and good work dynamics.

The first step to building an effective team is identifying the skills and competencies necessary for the project. What specific roles are required and what technical, creative or interpersonal skills are essential? Looking for people who not only meet the technical requirements, but also fit culturally with the team is key to building a solid foundation.

Once the necessary roles have been identified, it is important to recruit people who not only have the right skills, but also the motivation and commitment to the project. Look for individuals who are excited about the project goal and willing to collaborate effectively with other team members.

Communication is another fundamental aspect in building effective teams. It is crucial to establish clear and open channels of communication from the beginning. This includes ensuring that all team members understand their roles and responsibilities, as well as fostering an environment where they feel comfortable sharing ideas, concerns or suggestions.

In addition to communication, mutual trust is essential for an effective team. Members must trust the skills and competencies of their colleagues, as well as their commitment to the project objectives. Fostering an environment of respect and support helps build this trust, which in turn strengthens team cohesion and improves overall performance.

It's not just about individual skills; The ability to work as a team and collaborate effectively is crucial. This involves developing active listening skills, resolving conflict constructively, and leveraging individual strengths for the benefit of the team as a whole. Diversity of perspectives and skills can be a powerful asset if managed correctly.

Finally, building an effective team doesn't end once the right people have been recruited. It is important to invest in the continuous development of the team through training, regular feedback and celebrating the achievements achieved together. This helps maintain motivation and commitment throughout the project.

In short, building an effective team is essential to the success of any project. From identifying key skills to promoting open communication and building mutual trust, each step contributes to creating an environment where individual talent combines to achieve collective goals effectively and successfully.

Effective Resource Management

When you're working on a project, resources are like the tools you need to build something. They can be money, time, people, equipment or any other asset necessary to achieve your goals. Managing these resources effectively is essential to ensure that the project progresses smoothly and within established limits.

The first step in resource management is to identify what resources are necessary to carry out the project. This involves making a detailed list of all required items, from personnel to specific materials and any other tangible or intangible resources needed to complete the tasks.

Once you have identified the necessary resources, it is important to allocate them appropriately. This means ensuring that each resource is available at the right time and in the quantity needed to meet the project requirements. Allocating resources efficiently helps avoid delays and ensures that activities proceed as planned.

Time management is also a key part of resource management. Time is a limited and valuable resource, so it is crucial to plan and schedule activities in a way that maximizes its use. Setting clear, realistic deadlines for each task and keeping track of progress helps ensure the project stays on track.

In addition to allocating resources and managing time, resource optimization is essential for project efficiency. This involves using available resources as efficiently as possible, minimizing waste and maximizing performance. It may involve reusing resources where possible, looking for more economical or efficient options, and looking for synergies between different resources to improve overall results.

Continuous monitoring and control are key aspects of effective resource management. This involves regularly tracking resource usage, comparing actual progress with planned progress and adjusting allocations as necessary. Identifying and addressing issues early helps prevent major deviations and keeps the project on track for success.

Finally, risk management is also part of resource management. Identifying possible risks that may affect the availability or effective use of resources allows developing mitigation strategies to minimize their impact on the project.

In short, effective resource management is essential to the success of any project. From the identification and proper allocation of resources to optimization and continuous monitoring, each step contributes to maximizing efficiency and ensuring that the project moves effectively toward its objectives.

Development of an Action Plan

When you have a clear idea and have defined your objectives, the next step is to develop a detailed action plan. Think of the action plan as the map that will guide you step by step from the beginning to the final goal of your project. It's like planning a trip: you need to know where you want to go and how to get there.

The first step in developing an action plan is to break down your main objective into smaller, specific goals. This helps make the project more manageable and allows you to measure progress along the way. Each goal must be clear, achievable and have a defined deadline for its achievement.

Once you have your goals established, it is time to identify the specific actions you need to take to achieve each of them. This involves determining what specific tasks need to be completed, who will be responsible for each, and when they should be completed. The more detailed your action plan is, the easier it will be for you and your team to follow it and meet the established objectives.

In addition to specific actions, it is important to assign appropriate resources to each task. This includes not only material resources such as money or equipment, but also human resources, ensuring that the right people with the necessary skills are assigned to each task.

Sequencing activities is also key in developing an effective action plan. Determining the order in which tasks should be carried out and the dependencies between them helps you avoid bottlenecks and keep your workflow consistent. You can use tools like Gantt charts or calendars to visualize the sequence and duration of each task.

In addition to sequencing, it is essential to establish important checkpoints and milestones along the way. These are key moments where you can evaluate the progress of the project, review if you are on the right track, and make adjustments if necessary. Milestones also serve to celebrate achievements and motivate the team towards the next step.

Don't forget to also include a communication plan in your action plan. Effective communication within the team and with external stakeholders is crucial to keeping everyone informed and aligned with project goals. Define how information will be shared, who will be responsible for communication, and how often it will be updated.

Finally, a good action plan is not static, but should be flexible and adaptable as the project progresses. Unexpected changes or new challenges may arise, and being prepared to adjust the plan as necessary is key to maintaining effectiveness and efficiency in achieving your goals.

In short, developing an effective action plan is essential to turning your goals into reality. From defining clear goals to allocating resources, sequencing activities, setting milestones and communicating effectively, each step brings you closer to the success of your project.

Kevin Myers

Project Implementation and Execution

Getting to the implementation and execution phase is like bringing your project to life after a lot of planning and preparation work. It's time to put into practice everything you have planned and seen on paper. This stage is crucial because it is when you will really see if your project can become a reality and achieve the objectives you have set for yourself.

The first step in implementation is to ensure that all necessary resources are available and ready to use. This includes people, equipment, materials, and any other resources identified in your action plan. It is essential that everything is in place so that the project can begin as scheduled.

Once you have everything ready, begin executing the activities as established in your action plan. Each team member must clearly know what is expected of them and what their role is in the project. It is important to maintain open and regular communication to ensure that everyone is aligned and working towards the same goal.

During execution, it is crucial to monitor project progress closely. This involves tracking ongoing activities, comparing progress with the established plan, and resolving any issues or deviations that may arise. The ability to detect problems early and take corrective action is essential to keep the project on the right track.

In addition to monitoring progress, time management is essential during project execution. Maintaining the established schedule helps you meet deadlines and avoid delays that could affect the overall success of the project. It is important to be flexible but also diligent to ensure that each task is completed on time.

Risk management is also an integral part of project execution. As you progress, new challenges or unforeseen situations may arise that threaten the success of the project. Having contingency plans in place and being ready to adapt to changes helps you minimize negative impacts and maintain forward momentum.

In addition to technical implementation, it is crucial to keep team morale high. Recognizing and celebrating milestones achieved, as well as providing positive feedback and support where necessary, goes a long way to maintaining team motivation and engagement throughout the project.

Finally, effective communication should not be overlooked during implementation. Keeping all stakeholders informed of progress, achievements and challenges helps build trust and maintain the support necessary for project success.

In short, project implementation and execution is the moment when planning becomes action and your ideas begin to take shape. From initial preparation to monitoring progress, time management and problem solving, every step is crucial to ensuring your project moves effectively toward its end goals.

Risk and Contingency Management

When you are carrying out a project, there is always the possibility that something will turn out differently than you planned. That's where risk and contingency management comes in: it's like having a plan B ready in case unexpected problems arise that could affect the success of your project.

The first step in risk management is to identify what could go wrong. This involves identifying all possible risks that could arise during the execution of the project. Risks can be of different types, such as technical risks (such as equipment failure), financial risks (such as unexpected costs), operational risks (such as logistics problems) or external risks (such as changes in the market).

Once potential risks have been identified, it is important to evaluate the likelihood of them occurring and the impact they could have on the project if they materialize. Some risks may have minor consequences, while others could be critical and seriously affect the success of the project. This assessment helps you prioritize risks and decide where to focus your mitigation efforts.

After identifying and evaluating risks, the next step is to develop mitigation strategies. These strategies are preventative actions you can take to reduce the likelihood of identified risks occurring or to minimize their impact if they do occur. For example, you could implement additional quality controls, diversify suppliers, or establish reserve funds.

In addition to mitigation strategies, it is important to have contingency plans prepared. These are alternative plans that you can activate if a risk materializes and affects the project. Contingency plans must be clear, detailed and communicated to the entire team so that they know what to do and how to respond quickly to adverse situations.

During project execution, it is crucial to continually monitor identified risks and update your mitigation strategies as necessary. Risks can change over time due to external or internal factors, so it is important to be prepared to adjust your response plans as the situation evolves.

In addition to managing identified risks, it is important to be aware of emerging or new risks that may arise during the course of the project. Maintaining a proactive mindset and being prepared to deal with the unexpected is key to minimizing disruptions and keeping the project on track toward its goals.

In summary, risk and contingency management is a fundamental part of project management. From the initial identification of risks to the implementation of mitigation strategies and the preparation of contingency plans, each step helps you maintain control over the course of the project and increase the chances of success despite the challenges that may arise due to the project. path.

Monitoring and Control of Progress

When you're carrying out a project, it's not enough to just start and hope for the best. It is crucial to have a robust monitoring and control system to ensure that everything is progressing as planned and to be able to take corrective action if necessary. It's like being behind the wheel of a car: you need to watch the road constantly to make sure you're facing the right direction and adjust if necessary.

Progress monitoring involves closely monitoring how activities and tasks within the project are progressing. This means keeping an up-to-date record of work completed, milestones reached, and any deviations that may arise compared to the initial plan. Maintaining regular monitoring allows you to have a clear view of how the project is developing in real time.

Monitoring progress goes beyond simple monitoring: it involves taking actions based on the information collected during monitoring. If you identify that an activity is not progressing as expected or that there are delays in the delivery of certain results, it is important to intervene in a timely manner. This could involve allocating more resources, rescheduling tasks, or even revising the action plan if necessary.

A key part of monitoring and controlling progress is the comparison between what is planned and what is actual. This involves regularly analyzing whether you are meeting established deadlines, whether costs are within the planned budget, and whether the quality of work is as expected. Identifying gaps between plan and reality allows you to make informed decisions to keep the project on track toward its goals.

In addition to monitoring the progress of tasks, it is also important to evaluate the quality of the work performed. This involves ensuring that defined quality standards and criteria are met across all project deliverables and results. Quality is crucial to customer satisfaction and to ensure that the project generates the expected results.

Another fundamental aspect of monitoring and controlling progress is change management. As you progress through the project, new needs, opportunities, or challenges may arise that require adjustments to the original plan. Being able to manage these changes effectively and evaluate their impact on the project is key to adapting and responding agilely to changing circumstances.

Communication plays a crucial role in monitoring and controlling progress. It is important to keep all stakeholders informed about the current status of the project, achievements made, problems identified, and corrective actions taken. Clear, regular communication helps align expectations, maintain support, and ensure everyone is on the same page regarding project progress.

In summary, monitoring and controlling progress is essential to ensure the success of any project. From monitoring activities and comparing results with the original plan to taking corrective actions and managing changes, each step helps keep the project on track and maximize the chances of achieving established objectives.

Problem Solving and Decision Making

When you're working on a project, you're almost guaranteed to encounter challenges and problems along the way. Problem solving is like finding creative solutions to those obstacles to keep your project moving forward. It's like being a detective: you need to identify the problem, investigate the causes, and then find the best way to solve it.

The first step in problem solving is to clearly define what the problem is. Sometimes it may be obvious, such as a delay in the delivery of materials, but other times the problem may be hidden behind other symptoms. It is crucial to understand the root of the problem in order to address it effectively.

Once you have identified the problem, the next step is to analyze the underlying causes. This involves investigating what could have caused the problem in the first place. It may be due to errors in planning, lack of adequate resources, communication problems, or changes in external circumstances. Understanding the causes helps you avoid superficial solutions and address the problem holistically.

After understanding the problem and its causes, it is time to generate options to solve it. This involves thinking creatively and considering different possible approaches. You can consult the team, seek outside opinions, or explore solutions that have worked in similar situations. The more options you have, the more likely you are to find the best solution.

Once you have several options on the table, it's time to evaluate them carefully. Consider the pros and cons of each option, as well as its feasibility and potential impact on the project. It is also important to evaluate the risk associated with each option and how it could affect other parts of the project or stakeholders.

After evaluating the options, make an informed decision about which solution to implement. This may involve consulting with the team or relevant stakeholders before making the final decision. Make sure you clearly communicate the decision made and the reasons behind it to maintain transparency and trust in the team.

Once the solution is implemented, it is crucial to monitor the results and evaluate its effectiveness. This allows you to verify if the solution effectively resolved the issue or if additional adjustments are needed. Continuous feedback helps you learn from experience and improve your problem-solving skills for future challenges.

In addition to problem solving, effective decision making is also key throughout the project. This involves making decisions about resource allocation, adjustments to the action plan, change management, and other important issues that may arise. The ability to make informed and quick decisions goes a long way in keeping the project on track and achieving established objectives.

In short, problem solving and decision making are critical skills for any project manager. From identifying and understanding the problem to generating options, evaluating them, and making informed decisions, each step brings you closer to keeping the project on track and overcoming challenges that may arise on the path to success.

Kevin Myers

Effective Communication at all Levels

When it comes to carrying out a project, effective communication is like the glue that holds the entire team together and ensures that everyone is on the same page. It is like speaking a common language that allows you to transmit ideas, share information and solve problems clearly and efficiently.

First, effective communication begins with clarity in the message. It is important to express your ideas in a direct and understandable way, avoiding jargon or technicalities that could confuse your audience. This ensures that everyone correctly understands what is expected of them and what the objectives and goals of the project are.

In addition to clarity, effective communication also involves being concise and direct. This means conveying information succinctly and to the point, without unnecessary detours. Brevity not only saves time, but also makes it easier to understand and reduces the chance of misunderstanding.

Communication is not only about speaking, but also about active listening. It is important to be attentive to the concerns, ideas and suggestions of other team members and interested parties. Active listening not only fosters a collaborative environment, but also helps solve problems and make more informed decisions.

In addition to verbal communication, effective communication also includes the use of other means and tools. This can include emails, virtual meetings, project management tools, and instant messaging platforms. Using the appropriate medium based on the situation and communication needs ensures that information is transmitted effectively and in a timely manner.

Transparency is another key aspect of effective communication. Keeping everyone informed about project progress, challenges faced, and successes achieved helps build trust and maintain team commitment. Transparency also facilitates problem solving and decision making by allowing everyone to have access to the same information.

In addition to communication within the team, effective communication also involves external stakeholders. This may include customers, suppliers, partners, and other parties involved in the project. Maintaining clear and consistent communication with these parties ensures that all expectations are aligned and that any changes or adjustments are handled appropriately.

Conflict management is another area where effective communication plays a crucial role. It is natural for differences of opinion or conflicts to arise during the course of a project. Knowing how to handle these conflicts diplomatically and constructively through open and respectful communication helps maintain harmony within the team and maintain focus on the project's objectives.

Finally, feedback is essential to continually improve communication. Requesting and providing feedback regularly helps identify areas of improvement, strengths and weaknesses in communication within the team and with stakeholders. This promotes an environment of learning and growth where everyone can contribute to the success of the project.

In short, effective communication at all levels is an essential ingredient for the success of any project. From clarity and conciseness of message to active listening, transparency, conflict management and continuous feedback, each aspect contributes to creating a collaborative and efficient environment where ideas become actions and projects move towards success. .

Adaptation to Change and Flexibility

When you're working on a project, one thing you should always keep in mind is that things can change at any time. Adapting to change and flexibility is like being able to dance to music, adjusting when the melody changes to keep your pace moving forward.

One of the key aspects of adapting to change is open-mindedness. This means being prepared to accept that plans can change and being willing to adjust quickly based on circumstances. In a dynamic business and project world, rigidity can be your biggest enemy, while flexibility allows you to navigate challenges more effectively.

Communication plays a crucial role in adapting to change. It is important to keep everyone informed of any changes to the plan or circumstances that may affect the project. Clear and timely communication helps avoid misunderstandings and ensures that everyone is aligned on any adjustments that need to be made.

Being flexible also means being willing to learn and adapt to new situations and technologies. In an environment where innovation is constant, the ability to acquire new skills and knowledge allows you to stay relevant and effective in project execution. Being open to continuous learning better prepares you to face future changes with confidence.

In addition to being responsive to external changes, flexibility also refers to the ability to manage internal changes within the team and the organization. This may include adjustments to team structure, changes to roles and responsibilities, or modifications to processes and procedures to improve efficiency and effectiveness.

Resilience is another important skill associated with adapting to change. It means being able to quickly recover from setbacks or adverse situations and continue making progress toward project objectives. Resilience helps you stay positive and motivated even when things don't go as initially planned.

An effective strategy to facilitate adaptation to change is to have contingency plans prepared. These are backup plans that you can activate if unexpected problems arise or circumstances change drastically. Having alternative options gives you the ability to respond quickly and keep the project on track without major interruptions.

Finally, the ability to make quick and effective decisions is crucial for adapting to change. As new challenges or opportunities arise, being able to quickly assess the situation, consider options and make informed decisions allows you to maintain forward momentum and take advantage of new opportunities that may arise.

In summary, adaptation to change and flexibility are essential skills in the world of projects. From maintaining an open and communicative mindset to being resilient in the face of setbacks and being prepared with contingency plans, each aspect helps you manage challenges effectively and stay on track for project success, regardless of changes that may arise in the future. the way.

Evaluation and Continuous Improvement

When you're carrying out a project, it's not just about doing things once and hoping for the best. Continuous evaluation and improvement is like constantly reviewing your work to see how you can do it better. It's like polishing a diamond: always looking for ways to make it shine even more.

Evaluation begins with regular review of project progress. This involves looking closely at how objectives are being achieved, whether deadlines are being met, and whether the expected quality is being maintained. It is important to have clear, measurable indicators to evaluate performance and determine what is working well and what areas might need adjustments.

A key part of the evaluation is collecting both internal and external feedback. Listening to the opinions and comments of team members, clients, stakeholders, and other interested parties gives you invaluable insight into how they perceive the project and what areas could be improved. This feedback helps you identify blind spots and adjust your approach as necessary.

In addition to feedback, it is important to conduct periodic reviews of the process and procedures used in the project. This involves analyzing the effectiveness of the methods and tools used, identifying possible areas of inefficiency or redundancy, and exploring new techniques or technologies that can improve efficiency and results.

Continuous improvement also involves the ability to learn from mistakes and successes. Celebrating achievements and analyzing what contributed to your success helps replicate those elements in future projects. Likewise, identifying mistakes or areas for improvement gives you the opportunity to implement changes and avoid making the same mistakes in the future.

Implementing changes based on evaluation and feedback not only improves the current project, but also strengthens the team's skills and capabilities. Fostering a culture of continuous improvement promotes innovation and adaptability within the team, which is essential in a competitive and constantly changing business environment.

Technology plays an important role in continuous evaluation and improvement, providing tools and systems that facilitate data collection, performance analysis, and detailed reporting. Using these tools allows you to obtain a more accurate and objective view of the project's progress and facilitates making informed decisions for improvement.

Finally, continuous evaluation and improvement does not stop once the project is complete. It is important to apply these principles throughout the entire project life cycle, from planning to implementation and closure. This ensures that the project not only achieves its initial objectives, but also evolves and adapts as circumstances and business needs change.

In summary, continuous evaluation and improvement are essential to the sustained success of any project. From regularly reviewing progress and collecting feedback to implementing changes and applying advanced technology, each step contributes to strengthening the project and maximizing its results for the benefit of everyone involved.

Celebration of Achievements and Team Motivation

When you work on a project, it's not all about achieving goals; It is also important to recognize and celebrate the achievements made along the way. Celebrating achievements is like a boost of positive energy that motivates the team and strengthens the sense of camaraderie. It's like a reminder that the effort is worth it and that together you can achieve great things.

An effective way to celebrate achievements is to publicly recognize the team's successes. This may include team meetings where individual and collective achievements are highlighted, as well as the presentation of formal recognition such as awards or certificates. Recognizing hard work and positive results boosts team members' self-esteem and confidence.

Celebration can also take the form of simple but meaningful gestures, such as a special meal or recreational activity after reaching an important milestone. These informal celebrations foster a positive work environment and help build strong relationships between team members. Additionally, they offer a time of rest and relaxation that can revitalize the team for future challenges.

Another way to celebrate achievements is to share success with the entire organization or relevant stakeholders. This can be through internal communications, newsletters, or even presentations at corporate events. Sharing achievements not only recognizes the team's work, but also strengthens the image and reputation of the project within the organization and beyond.

Team motivation is also crucial to maintaining momentum and commitment throughout the project. In addition to celebrating accomplishments, it's important to regularly communicate the importance of each team member's work and how they contribute to the overall success of the project. This helps keep morale high and strengthen the sense of purpose and connection to organizational goals.

An effective leader plays a key role in celebrating achievements and motivating the team. This involves not only recognizing achievements, but also actively inspiring and supporting team members. The ability to listen, guide, and provide constructive feedback is critical to cultivating a positive and productive work environment.

In addition to celebrating present achievements, it is also important to set future goals and challenges to keep the team motivated and focused on continued growth. Setting achievable but ambitious goals creates a sense of direction and provides opportunities to continue celebrating new achievements as they are achieved.

In short, celebrating achievements and motivating the team are essential components to the success of any project. From publicly recognizing successes to sharing success with the organization and maintaining motivation through effective communication and engaged leadership, each aspect contributes to strengthening the team and creating an environment where everyone feels valued and motivated to reach new heights.

Marketing and Promotion Strategies

When you have a project or a product that you want to be known and valued, marketing and promotion strategies are like the tools that help you make it shine and stand out in the market. It's like telling the world how great your project is and why they should pay attention to it.

One of the basic strategies is to know your target audience. This involves understanding who your potential customers are, what needs they have, and how your project can solve those needs. The better you understand your audience, the more effective your marketing strategies will be.

Branding is another fundamental aspect of marketing. This involves creating a unique and recognizable identity for your project, including the name, logo, colors and visual style. Strong branding helps differentiate your project from the competition and build an emotional connection with your clients.

Once you are clear about who your audience is and how you want to be perceived, you can begin to develop communication strategies.

This includes deciding which communication channels you will use to reach your audience, such as social media, online advertising, email, events, and more. Each channel has its advantages and it is important to choose the ones that best suit your target audience and budget.

Creating relevant and valuable content is another key strategy in digital marketing. This can include blog articles, video tutorials, infographics, podcasts, and more. Providing useful content not only helps educate your audience about your project, but also positions your brand as an authority in your field.

Paid advertising can also be part of your marketing strategy. This includes ads on social networks like Facebook and Instagram, search ads on Google, and collaborations with influencers. Paid advertising allows you to quickly reach a specific audience and can be effective in generating brand recognition and direct sales.

Word-of-mouth marketing remains powerful even in the digital age. This is achieved through recommendations and reviews from satisfied customers, testimonials on your website, and referral programs. Trust among consumers is strengthened when they see that others have had positive experiences with your project.

Data analysis is crucial to evaluate the effectiveness of your marketing strategies. This involves monitoring key metrics such as website traffic, conversions, social media engagement, and the return on investment (ROI) of your campaigns. With this data, you can continually adjust and optimize your strategies for better results.

Finally, consistency and adaptability are important in marketing. Maintaining a consistent presence on selected channels and being prepared to adjust your strategies as market trends and needs evolve will help you maintain relevance and success in the long term.

In short, marketing and promotion strategies are essential to take your project to the next level. From understanding your audience and developing strong branding to using multiple communication channels and analyzing data to continually improve, each step brings you closer to achieving your business goals and making your project stand out in a competitive market.

Kevin Myers

Financial Management and Budget

When you're working on a project, financial management is like managing money wisely to make sure everything runs smoothly and within budget. It's like having a map that guides you on how and where to spend every penny to get the best possible results.

The first step in financial management is to create a detailed budget. This involves estimating all costs involved in the project, from materials and equipment to professional fees and operating expenses. A clear budget helps you plan and control expenses throughout the project, avoiding unpleasant financial surprises.

It is also important to establish priorities within the budget. This means identifying which areas or activities are critical to the success of the project and allocating resources appropriately. Sometimes this can involve making difficult decisions about where to invest more and where to adjust to stay within budget limits.

Cash flow management is another crucial aspect of financial management. This involves monitoring and managing income and expenses in real time to ensure that there is always enough cash available to cover the operational needs of the project. Maintaining positive cash flow is essential to avoid liquidity problems that may affect project execution.

In addition to daily cash management, it is important to consider long-term planning. This includes financial projections that estimate the future income and expenses of the project. Projections help you anticipate future financial needs and make informed decisions about investments and financing.

Proper accounting is essential for effective financial management. This involves maintaining accurate and up-to-date records of all financial transactions related to the project. A solid accounting system provides you with clear and detailed financial information that facilitates decision making and compliance with tax obligations.

Evaluating return on investment (ROI) is another important component of financial management. This involves analyzing the benefits obtained in relation to the costs incurred in the project. Determining ROI helps you evaluate the efficiency and effectiveness of your investments and adjust strategies if necessary to maximize results.

Financial risk management must also be considered. This involves identifying potential risks that could affect project finances, such as changes in material costs, market fluctuations, or regulatory changes. Developing risk mitigation strategies helps you protect project financial resources and minimize potential losses.

Finally, transparency and communication are key in financial management. Keeping all stakeholders informed about the financial status of the project and any challenges that may arise fosters trust and collaboration. Open communication also makes it easier to identify financial problems early and allows corrective action to be taken quickly.

In summary, effective financial management and a well-planned budget are essential to the success of any project. From creating a detailed budget and cash flow management to accurate accounting and ROI evaluation, every aspect contributes to maintaining the financial health of the project and ensuring that established objectives are achieved without compromising financial stability.

Sustainability and Future of the Project

When we talk about sustainability in a project, we refer to its ability to last and be beneficial in the long term, both for the environment and for society. It's about making sure that what we are doing today does not compromise the opportunities and resources of future generations.

A fundamental part of sustainability is considering the environmental impact of our actions. This involves minimizing the use of natural resources, reducing waste and emissions, and adopting practices that protect the environment. For example, using recycled or renewable materials in the construction or production of a project can significantly reduce its ecological footprint.

In addition to environmental impact, sustainability also encompasses social and economic impact. This involves ensuring that the project contributes positively to the well-being of the local community and promotes social equity. For example, involving local communities in project development and providing employment and training opportunities can have a lasting positive impact.

Long-term planning is essential to ensure the sustainability of a project. This involves considering how decisions made today will affect the project in the future. For example, designing infrastructure that can adapt to climate or technological changes ensures that the project remains relevant and effective for decades to come.

Innovation plays a crucial role in sustainability. Adopting new technologies and practices that are more efficient in the use of resources and less harmful to the environment can significantly improve the sustainability of a project. For example, the integration of renewable energy or the use of water conservation technologies can reduce long-term operating costs and improve the environmental image of the project.

Education and awareness are key to promoting sustainability among all those involved in the project. This includes everyone from workers and suppliers to customers and the community in general. Training people about sustainable practices and the benefits of adopting them can foster a cultural change that lasts beyond the current project.

In addition to environmental and social benefits, sustainability can also have economic advantages. For example, reducing energy and water consumption can lower long-term operating costs and improve project profitability. Furthermore, more and more consumers and companies prefer to partner with projects that demonstrate a clear commitment to sustainability, which can open up new business and market opportunities.

It is important to regularly evaluate and measure project performance in terms of sustainability. This involves establishing clear indicators and achievable goals that allow progress towards sustainability to be monitored over time. Transparency in reporting on project environmental and social performance also builds trust and credibility among all stakeholders.

In short, sustainability is not just a trend, but a pressing need in modern project management. From consideration of environmental and social impact to long-term planning and adoption of innovative technologies, every step we take towards sustainability contributes to ensuring a better, more resilient future for our projects and the world at large.

www.ingramcontent.com/pod-product-compliance
Lightning Source LLC
Chambersburg PA
CBHW020642160726
47991CB00003B/982